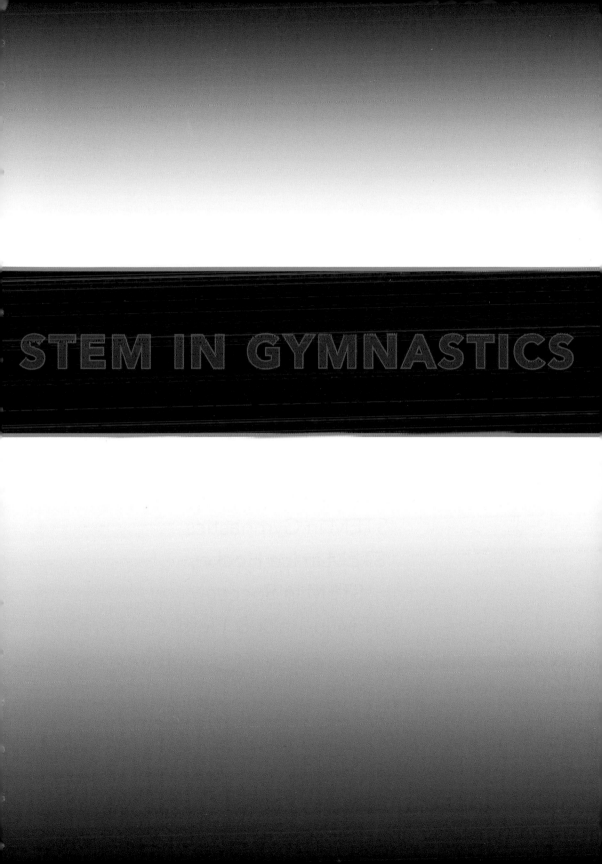

STEM IN GYMNASTICS

CONNECTING
STEM AND SPORTS

CONNECTING
STEM
AND SPORTS

STEM IN GYMNASTICS

JACQUELINE HAVELKA

MASON CREST
PHILADELPHIA · MIAMI

Mason Crest
450 Parkway Drive, Suite D
Broomall, Pennsylvania 19008
(866) MCP-BOOK (toll free)

First printing
9 8 7 6 5 4 3 2 1

ISBN (hardback) 978-1-4222-4335-0
ISBN (series) 978-1-4222-4329-9
ISBN (ebook) 978-1-4222-7479-8

Cataloging-in-Publication Data on file with the Library of Congress

Developed and Produced by National Highlights Inc.
Editor: Andrew Luke
Interior and cover design: Annalisa Gumbrecht, Studio Gumbrecht
Production: Michelle Luke

QR CODES AND LINKS TO THIRD-PARTY CONTENT

TABLE OF CONTENTS

KEY ICONS TO LOOK FOR:

Words To Understand: These words with their easy-to-understand definitions will increase the reader's understanding of the text while building vocabulary skills.

Sidebars: This boxed material within the main text allows readers to build knowledge, gain insights, explore possibilities, and broaden their perspectives by weaving together additional information to provide realistic and holistic perspectives.

Educational Videos: Readers can view videos by scanning our QR codes, providing them with additional educational content to supplement the text. Examples include news coverage, moments in history, speeches, iconic sports moments, and much more!

Text-Dependent Questions: These questions send the reader back to the text for more careful attention to the evidence presented there.

Research Projects: Readers are pointed toward areas of further inquiry connected to each chapter. Suggestions are provided for projects that encourage deeper research and analysis.

Series Glossary Of Key Terms: This back-of-the-book glossary contains terminology used throughout this series. Words found here increase the reader's ability to read and comprehend higher-level books and articles in this field.

INTRODUCTION

Macaroni and cheese. Texting and emojis. STEM and sports. What? STEM—and sports? Yes! When one thinks about STEM classes and sports, they seem like opposites, right? You're either in the classroom learning, or you're on the playing field.

But STEM and sports really do go together. STEM is education in four specific areas—science, technology, engineering, and mathematics. Rather than being taught as separate subjects, STEM curriculum is integrated together for real-world learning. When a science class visits an amusement park, the students learn the principles of physics, use math to make calculations, and learn about the engineering and technology used to construct roller coasters and other rides.

Gymnastics is a sport that requires athletic strength and skill as well as artistic beauty, but it is also a sport that exemplifies science and energy. Newton's laws of physics definitely apply to gymnastics.

⬦ Newton's First Law: An object at rest stays at rest. In order to move, an external force must act on it. This defines the law of inertia.

⬦ Newton's Second Law of Motion defines the famous $F=ma$ equation. This law says that the force of an object is equal to its mass multiplied by its acceleration.

⬦ Newton's Third Law of Motion states that for every action, there is an equal and opposite reaction.

Gymnasts make some amazing gravity-defying moves, but you might be surprised to find out there is lots of science behind those vaults and balance beam routines. Let's take a look at the STEM concepts in gymnastics. We'll explore concepts, like force, inertia, acceleration, and projectile motion—all important to the sport.

CHAPTER 1

EVOLUTION OF GYMNASTICS

Introduction

The sport of gymnastics has definitely changed over the last three decades. Floor routines have become much harder, incorporating complex tumbling routines. The vault is higher and now rectangular so that gymnasts can make gravity-defying moves. The uneven bars are now farther apart, which greatly complicates the moves gymnasts must make. Even balance beam routines incorporate more difficult skills these days.

International standards for the sport were developed in the 1950s, and clear guidelines were developed for women and men. One of the biggest changes came

Olga Korbut changed the sport of gymnastics by shifting the focus from artistry to athleticism.

in the 1972 Olympic games, when spectators were shocked to see gymnast Olga Korbut of the former Soviet Union, who was less about grace and more about strength and power. It was a stunning change for the sport.

 Olga Korbut

Who is Olga Korbut? She is a gymnast from the former Soviet Union who won six Olympic medals—four gold and two silver—at the 1972 Munich and 1976 Montreal Olympic Games. She was also the first gymnast inducted into the International Gymnastics Hall of Fame, in 1988. As a gymnast, Korbut revolutionized the sport of gymnastics. She has been named by *Sports Illustrated* as one of the forty greatest athletes of all time. She brought high-level acrobatics and raw strength to the sport and was responsible for inspiring many young girls to take up gymnastics. Prior to Korbut, gymnasts were generally much older, and the sport focused on elegance rather than athleticism. Korbut retired from gymnastics in 1977 at the old age of twenty-two. She is in her mid-sixties now, lives in Arizona, and is still active in the sport of gymnastics by performing speaking engagements and other duties.

Physicality of the Sport

The sport has never been the same since Korbut, and science shows why gymnastics is probably the most difficult sport on the planet. Some of the skills that gymnasts need to perform follow:

- Balance.

- Rotation—in less than one second, gymnasts can do 900 or 1080 degrees of rotation in twisting moves.

- Spatial awareness, proprioception, and **kinesthetic awareness**.

- Accuracy in timing, to 6/1000 of a second.

- Male gymnasts have to have a short-distance sprint speed of twenty or more miles per hour (sixteen for women).

- Men and women reach tumbling and vault heights of sixteen and thirteen feet high, respectively.

- To perform some of these athletic moves, gymnasts have to have the strength to momentarily handle loads of force up to nine times their body weight. That's amazing!

Scoring

Gymnasts need speed, **agility**, strength, power, flexibility, **hand-eye coordination**, and analytical ability to calculate twists and landings. Famous Romanian gymnast Nadia Comaneci scored the first perfect 10 in the 1976 Olympic Games. To the crowd's amazement, Comaneci went on to achieve seven perfect 10s to become the world's new gymnastics sensation.

The relative strength of world-class gymnasts is among the highest of any athletes in the world.

Twenty years later, after so many gymnasts were achieving perfect 10s, the International Federation of Gymnastics changed the scoring system to make a 10 more difficult to achieve.

Today, gymnasts continue to exhibit unbelievable skills. They've become more athletic, so the scoring system was recently changed once again after the 2004 Olympic Games to involve a very complex judging procedure. In today's sport, you'll no longer see the perfect 10.

Gymnasts now get two scores in a scoring system officially known as "the Code of Points." One score is for execution (E-score), and gymnasts can earn up to 10 points. The other score is for degree of difficulty (D-score), and gymnasts rarely earn higher than a 6.5. That's because the International Federation has

I love it, but I don't understand it. This video offers a simple explanation of how gymnastics is scored under the new system.

left some growing room in the degree of difficulty score. The top score today is 16.5—a perfect routine executed at the top degree of difficulty. However, no gymnast has yet achieved an execution score of 10.

Why Did the Scoring Change?

The old scoring system rewarded athletes who did the math and played it safe. Tiny fractions, such as 9.87 versus 9.91 could make the difference between a gold and silver medal. The International Federation of Gymnastics decided a change was needed.

Innovators in the sport have and always will attempt more difficult tricks, particularly when scoring rewards for it. Judges wanted a way to reward people for pushing the sport forward

Modern gymnastics rewards athletes for the difficulty of the routine more so than for a flawless execution.

by trying these new feats, even if the tricks were not performed perfectly. Therefore, judges developed the two scores to reward strength and speed. The "perfect 10" system rewarded an easy routine performed perfectly, and now the new scoring system rewards gymnasts for attempting harder routines.

Fans are not as happy, because it was easier to understand scores on a basis of 10, but fans will likely be won over as they see how the sport progresses in the next few years. Of course, many in the gymnastics world would like to see the scoring revert back to the old way.

The U.S. women's team are the current two-time defending Olympic champions in the team all-around event.

However, that seems very unlikely, and the new system is really not that hard to understand. Also, gymnastics is more popular than it has ever been, particularly in the United States, because U.S. women have won the gold medal in the all-around competition at the last two Olympic Games. Gymnastics is more athletic than ever.

The new scoring system has focused gymnasts more on defying gravity in their vaults and tumbling. Let's explore the physics behind those gravity-defying moves, shall we?

Olympic champion Aliya Mustafina soars off the vault at the 2016 Olympic games in Rio de Janeiro.

Text-Dependent Questions:

1. What physical skills make gymnastics the most difficult sport to physically execute?

2. What are Olga Korbut and Nadia Comaneci famous for?

3. Why did judges create the new gymnastics scoring system?

Research Project:

If a full revolution of a gymnast's body is 360 degrees, calculate how many full body turns are involved in both 900 degree turns and 1080-degree turns. If these moves happen in less than a second, also calculate how long each full 360-degree body revolution takes in each instance. Do some research to compare your findings to rotation speeds in other sports, like snowboarding or figure skating. Who are the speediest spinners?

WORDS TO UNDERSTAND

center of gravity: the point through which the resultant gravitational forces on a body passes and from which the resultant force of attraction of the body on other bodies flows out

center of mass: the point in the body where all the mass of the body is concentrated

inertia: the property of matter by which it retains its state of rest or its velocity along a straight line so long as an external force does not act upon it

CHAPTER 2

BALANCE EVENTS: CENTER OF MASS

Introduction

Gymnastics requires balance, strength, and technique. Athletes push the limits on physics when they perform these amazing feats. Balance is a core element for almost any gymnastics routine—floor tumbling, parallel bars, vault, or beam. One of the first skills that any gymnast will develop is learning to maintain balance in a variety of body positions.

Gymnasts learn why they do or do not remain balanced in different positions, then they practice drills to improve their balancing skills. What does physics have to do with this? It's all about stabilizing your **center of gravity**.

Gravity

We tend to think about gravity as a force that pulls objects downward—"what goes up must come down," right? Gravity also makes things topple over, however, particularly objects that are unbalanced—like a gymnast. Think of a tightrope

Most gymnasts, like 5'2" Olympic champion Gabby Douglas of the US, tend to be short, both men and women. Short people are generally more successful at gymnastics due to having a low center of gravity.

walker: They're moving slowly on the high wire, always wobbling from side to side. Tightrope walkers and gymnasts have lots in common. For example, they both understand the physics concept of center of gravity. By the way, for the purposes of this discussion, center of gravity and **center of mass** are the same. If we were on another planet where the gravity force was different, these two would also be different.

So what is center of gravity? What does it mean? If you throw a ball straight in the air, it comes straight back down. Most objects, like gymnasts, are more complexly shaped, but all objects respond to gravity as if their mass is concentrated at a single point in their body. This is called center of gravity. For simple objects like a round ball, finding the center of gravity is easy—it's in the center of the ball. In a human body the center of gravity rests slightly higher, above the waist, because the top half of your body weighs more than the bottom half. Gymnasts know this.

This explains why tall people topple over when they're unbalanced. If you stand up straight and begin leaning forward or to one side, you reach a point where you feel like you're going to fall. Your ankles are planted, so you are actually turning (pivoting) around your ankles. This is similar to a door on hinges. Stand with a door open, and push on it with one finger near the door handle. The door can freely pivot on its hinges. Now push on the door right next to the hinges. It's harder, isn't it? This is because you are closer to the pivot point.

Front and center—Watch this video that explains center of gravity.

It's the same for people. The taller the person, the more they'll pivot or turn. The taller the gymnast, the easier it is to topple over compared to a shorter gymnast, who is closer to the ground. As long as your center of gravity remains above your feet, you won't tip over. When you start to lean to the side or forward, your center of gravity is closer and closer to your feet and is no longer

Racecars are built low to the ground for the same reason gymnasts tend to be-having a low center of gravity is ideal.

at your midpoint. The more you lean, the more turning force your body has. Your whole body is rotating around your ankles.

The best way to maintain balance is to lower your center of gravity. Compare sitting to standing. When you're sitting, your center of gravity is much lower, and you are able to lean over more without falling. Did you ever wonder why race cars are so low to the ground? Now you know! A low center of gravity keeps the car from tipping no matter how fast it is going.

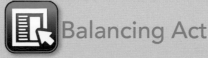 ## Balancing Act

You can do exercises to improve your balance, just like a gymnast does. Here are two drills gymnasts do.

1. **Flat-Footed Drill**
   Place your feet shoulder-width apart, and point your toes forward. Lift one foot, and keep it in the air. Hold your position for two seconds, and then return your foot to the floor. Repeat with the other foot. Do one or two sets of ten to twelve repetitions with each foot.

2. **Hopping Drill**
   Gymnasts must remain balanced while landing on one or two feet when executing dismounts and during floor routines, so they use this drill to develop the skill. Simply hop from one foot to the other. Start with the right foot flat on the floor. Flex that knee, and put your left foot in the air. Hop as high as you can off your right foot. Land on your left, flat-footed. Perform one or two sets of eight to ten repetitions while hopping off of each leg.

Balance

Gymnasts learn to use balancing aids. If you've ever watched a balance beam performance, you'll notice the gymnast holding her arms out to the side or bending her knees to get lower on the beam. All of these techniques give the gymnast more control over her center of gravity. The goal is to keep the gymnast's center of gravity directly over the beam at all times.

As the name suggests, balance is the name of the game on the beam.

If that happens, she is less likely to fall off. You will notice that gymnasts who teeter from side to side start to topple because the turning force pulls them in that direction. Gymnasts must very quickly compensate for that movement by moving part of their body to the other side to create a turning force in the opposite direction and therefore restore their balance.

Newton's law of **inertia** also factors in. Inertia is the tendency for objects at rest to stay at rest and objects in motion to stay in motion. Gymnasts are constantly compensating for their movements while on the beam. If she feels herself tipping, the gymnast has enough time to move another part of the body to the other side of the beam. Even though the gymnast may

Keeping a wide base of support makes it easier to maintain balance.

appear to be still on the beam, these forces are acting on her body. If an arm is out to her left side, gravity is acting on it, making her tip left. If the gymnast raises her right arm, then she creates a balancing force. It's not that the forces are not there. They are, but the left and right forces (sum of the forces) are canceling each other out, so the gymnast stays perfectly upright on the beam.

It's amazing to think about everything a gymnast must do to keep his or her center of gravity stable. On a floor routine, it is much easier to maintain a stable center of gravity on a wide, flat surface. It becomes exponentially more difficult on a balance beam, which is less than four inches wide. The gymnast is continually shifting her weight over the beam, all the while trying to maintain a stable center of gravity.

Another trick gymnasts use is to maintain a wide base of support, which is more stable than a narrow base. You can test this for yourself. Stand with your feet together, and lean to your right or left. Your body will easily be thrown off balance. Now place your feet shoulder width apart and lean. It is much easier for you to maintain your balance. The balance beam is so challenging because it prevents the gymnast from placing their feet apart. Notice, however, that when gymnasts dismount off the beam and land, their feet are usually apart.

Another great example of gymnasts' ability to maintain center of gravity is the still rings event. Male gymnasts certainly need massive upper body strength to successfully perform on the

Watch the amazing strength it takes for a gymnast to perform on the still rings. You can actually see how much force is acting on the gymnast's body.

If a gymnast competing on the rings does not have his center of mass perfectly aligned, his body will swing like a pendulum.

rings, but they also need to develop a very fine sense of balance to achieve and hold the correct body position.

The gymnast must keep his body in just the right position on the rings to hold himself stationary. To pull this off, the gymnast must be keenly aware of where his center of mass is located so that he can stay still.

If any force is applied directly to the center of mass, the object will not rotate about any axis. An unbalanced force, however, will set the object (in this case, the gymnast) rotating about the center of mass.

It might be easier to think of the gymnast's body as a pendulum. If you move a pendulum sideways and then let it go, it will swing. If the gymnast wants to remain still, the center of mass of his body must be right underneath the pivot points of the ring cables. If his center of mass is not aligned, the gymnast will swing just like the pendulum. Gymnasts are certainly strong, but swinging has nothing to do with overall strength. No matter how rigid his body is, if his center of mass is off, he will swing until the center of mass finally lies just below the pivot point of the ring. Hanging straight down on the rings is much easier than extending the arms straight out at ninety degrees and trying to maintain balance. It takes incredible strength.

Text-Dependent Questions:

1. Why do gymnasts need to learn to balance their center of gravity over the balance beam?

2. Why is a wider base of support more stable for maintaining center of gravity?

3. How do the door and pendulum examples teach us about center of gravity?

Research Project:

Do your own center of gravity investigation. Hang an object from a point on its edge. The object will rotate until its center of gravity is located directly under that point. Hang a weight on a string (called a plumb line) from the same point. Draw a line parallel to the string. Now pick a different point on the edge and repeat the process. Draw another line parallel to the string in a different color than the first line. The object's center of gravity is the point where the two lines meet.

WORDS TO UNDERSTAND

angular momentum: the product of the moment of inertia of a body about an axis and its angular velocity with respect to the same axis

axis of rotation: the central line about which a rotating body turns

momentum: force or speed of movement; impetus

CHAPTER 3

GYMNASTICS AND CONSERVATION OF ANGULAR MOMENTUM

Introduction

The physics of rotation plays a large part in the movement of a gymnast. As the gymnast runs across the mat, he gains speed. Mass, velocity, and distance all factor into **angular momentum**. At the moment he pushes off the mat, he has all the angular **momentum** he will have. It cannot be lost or gained, but gymnasts learn to change their rate of rotation while they are in the air.

How is this possible? The gymnast knows that if he changes the distance between his center of mass and the **axis of rotation**, he can change the angular speed and that changes the rate of rotation.

If you've ever seen a gymnast on the uneven parallel bars, you've seen this concept. The axis of rotation is the bar itself. The gymnast extends her full body away from the bar by holding on with her hands and hanging her feet down to the floor. She does a full body swing or two around the bar to gain

The uneven bars event perfectly demonstrates how changing angular speed changes rate of rotation.

angular momentum. As her hands leave the bar, this is all the angular momentum she will have. She will not gain or lose any, but then, she tucks her body into a ball. She is still spinning about the same axis even though the bar is not there, but tucking decreases the distance between her center of mass and the axis of rotation. You know what happens next—she begins spinning much faster even though her angular momentum has been constant.

Angular Momentum

Angular momentum is an interesting physics concept that is illustrated on the uneven bars, high bar, and trampoline. While the gymnast is in the air, only gravity is acting on her body (we are assuming that there is little to no air resistance).

Since the force of gravity is pulling straight down on her body, there is no external force that would cause her to twist or not rotate about that same axis. There is only the angular momentum around the center of mass.

In the uneven bars or high bar events, the axis of rotation is parallel with the floor. The gymnast can rotate about that axis head over feet as if doing a somersault around that axis. The direction of rotation is always perpendicular to the axis of rotation. The axis angle is zero, meaning that the body is not tilted about the axis.

The same example can be demonstrated with a spinning ice skater. This time, the skater is on a different axis; he is spinning about a vertical (y-) axis. Just like the gymnast builds up speed running across the mat, the skater builds up speed skating across the ice. As soon as his skates leave the ice, he achieves all the angular momentum possible. As the spin begins, only gravity is pulling down along the vertical axis. The skater also experiences some friction with the ice, but not much, so the spin will continue for a while. If the skater pulls his arms in, the spin gets faster, not because the skater has gained angular momentum but because the distance has narrowed between the center of gravity and the axis of rotation.

Gymnasts know how to change body position as they are spinning. They might start in a somersault, then they do a move called the "throw" technique. As they rotate, they move the left arm up and the right arm down (or vice versa). In response, the body tilts in the opposite direction, meaning the body tilts at an angle to the horizontal (x-) axis.

The high bar event demonstrates angular momentum, as the gymnast rotates around the axis of the bar.

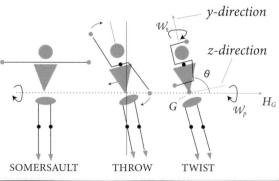

SOMERSAULT   THROW   TWIST

If the gymnast then bends both arms at the elbow, one arm will bend above her head and the other arm will be bent at her chest or waist. The body will then twist along a new vertical (y-) axis. Picture the y-axis coming out of the gymnast's head. It's really cool because at the same time, the gymnast is still rotating about the original x-axis. Rotation about both the x- and y-axes creates those amazing twisting moves we see gymnasts do.

Tucking the arms allows gymnasts to spin faster around the y-axis when attempting twisting maneuvers.

Regardless of the complexity of her moves, the gymnast is always rotating about her center of mass, and that is determined by Newton's $F=ma$ law because gravity is the only force acting on her body.

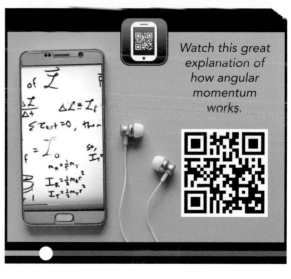

Watch this great explanation of how angular momentum works.

Another example is a gymnast on a trampoline. Using the same angular momentum principles, she can change her body orientation in midair simply by changing the position of her arms and legs. Here is an example.

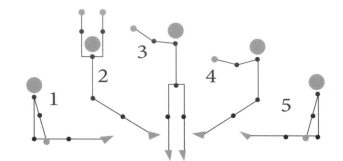

The trampoline event is another example of the concept of angular momentum.

If a gymnast wants to go from position 1 to position 5, she can do a series of movements to reach that position.

1. Bounce from a sitting position.

2. Raise her arms over her head by bringing them forward and up. The gymnast then rotates her upper body to turn her arms and shoulders as far around as possible, then drops her legs. At this point, the inertia in the lower body is large relative to the inertia in the top of the body, so the legs don't rotate.

3. Bring the arms forward and down. Swivel the hips beneath the extended arms. Now the lower body inertia is smaller than the upper body inertia.

4. Bring the feet and legs up.

5. End up in the sitting position facing the opposite way of position 1.

The Amanar

The Amanar vault is a difficult vault that really demonstrates angular momentum and twisting. The gymnast approaches the vault by doing a roundoff back handspring onto the vault and a flip off of the vault. This vault is named for Simona Amanar, the Romanian gymnast who first performed the difficult maneuver in the 2000 Olympic Games. Amanar is one of the best vaulters of all time. Since then, the American women's team has made the Amanar vault their signature move. It has been key to their major wins since 2011.

Check out an Amanar in action.

When a gymnast, like West Virginia University's Mackenzie Myers, is spinning, her angular momentum will not change unless acted on by a force other than gravity.

In conclusion, here are the key takeaway concepts. When an object is spinning and only gravity is acting on it (e.g., no external torque), the object will not have a change in angular momentum.

The conservation of angular momentum can be explained by the ice skater example of bringing her arms in. Since the angular momentum must remain constant (meaning that it must be conserved), she spins faster because she is decreasing the distance between the axis and her center of mass.

Text-Dependent Questions:

1. Does the direction of spin always occur perpendicular to the axis of rotation? Why or why not?

2. What happens when a gymnast is rotating and decreases the distance between the axis of rotation and his or her center of mass?

3. What is the "throw" technique?

Research Project:

With an adult's permission and supervision, perform the trampoline moves 1 to 5 as illustrated earlier. Record your observations, and report on what you learn about angular momentum.

WORDS TO UNDERSTAND

kinetic energy: energy associated with motion

potential energy: the energy of a body or system as a result of its position in an electric, magnetic, or gravitational field

rotational speed: the speed of an object rotating around an axis, often measured by the number of turns the object makes in a given period of time (i.e., revolutions per minute)

CHAPTER 4

HIGH BAR PHYSICS: THE GYMNASTICS GIANT

Introduction

Have you heard of the gymnastics giant? No, it does not refer to a really tall gymnast! Instead, the giant is a move gymnasts use on the high bar to increase their **rotational speed** before they dismount. The gymnast is hanging down by his arms from the high bar. In this position, he is at maximum height. Now imagine his body swinging 360 degrees around that bar. This is the gymnastics giant. Gymnasts often do it to pick up speed before they do another complex move on the bar.

In this skill, the gymnast rotates 360 degrees around the axis of the high bar while in a fully extended position. It is an impressive feat to watch on the male high bar. Female gymnasts also perform it on the uneven bars, and it is even done on the men's still rings event.

Doing the Giant

To do the move, the gymnast begins in a handstand position. With his legs together and his body fully extended, his feet descend. On the upswing, he uses his abdominal muscles to slightly arch the body so that the strength of the rotation is not affected. He can return to the handstand position, do another giant, or transition to another element. This is a difficult move because the

A gymnast warms up by performing a giant on the high bar.

gymnast must remain in the fully extended position for the entire giant move.

Think of the gymnast's body as a stick pivoting about a point (the point at which his hands are holding the bar). For the gymnast to swing faster, he must add energy to the system. He can do this by exerting a force as his center of mass moves around the bar.

Watch this breakdown of what it takes to compete on the horizontal bar, which includes doing several giants.

After the gymnast reaches the lowest point, he bends his legs, thus moving his body's center of mass closer to the center of rotation. This move is not easy to accomplish. Because his center of mass is moving in a circle, a force is needed to move the center of mass closer to the center of rotation. The gymnast must pull even more and that equates to the increase in energy. Where does this energy come from? It comes from the gymnast's muscles, which have **potential energy**. As he begins moving and pulling, the potential energy becomes **kinetic energy**, which is transferred into the rotational motion.

To keep gaining speed, which is the goal in the giant move, the gymnast must constantly reset his position because he must still add energy to gain more speed. This is best done at the highest point of the giant move. Once reset, he is back in the starting position but is going faster.

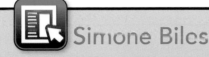 Simone Biles

Is Ohio native Simone Biles the greatest gymnast ever? Fellow gymnasts describe Biles as a "once-in-a-lifetime sort of gymnast" and the "kind of athlete the international judges had in mind" when they went to the new scoring system. Biles has amazing natural talent and perfectly and precisely performs skills that are unthinkable for other gymnasts. She has been described as having a "daredevil brand of gymnastics." She is, in a word, fearless. She even won nationals with broken toes—on both feet. After Biles completed at the 2016 Olympic Games in Rio de Janeiro, she stepped away from gymnastics as the best gymnast the world had ever seen. After a one-year hiatus, Biles returned to gymnastics in March 2018, even better than before. Biles is the first gymnast to win three consecutive World All-Around titles, and has the most World Championship gold medals of any female gymnast in history. She trains thirty-five hours per week.

Energy

Simone Biles waves to the crowd at the medal ceremony for one of four gold medals she won at the 2016 Olympic games in Rio de Janeiro.

Potential and kinetic energy definitely factor into gymnastics in a big way. Potential energy is the amount of energy an object gains through gravity acceleration, whereas kinetic energy is the amount of energy an object has when moving. Energy cannot be created or destroyed; instead it just changes form. This concept is known as the law of conservation of energy. Energy is constantly converted between the two forms: potential and kinetic energy.

The high bar is made of flexible composite material, so rather than being stiff, the bar does flex. This flexibility allows gymnasts to transfer energy between their body and the bar. They need that extra flex when they do difficult moves like the giant.

Watch the mind-blowing athleticism of Simone Biles.

During the gymnastics giant, when the gymnast is at the highest point in the air, he is motionless or nearly motionless. At this point, kinetic energy is the lowest, and potential energy is at its highest. At his lowest point, as he comes down toward the ground, the potential energy is at its lowest, and kinetic energy is at its highest. The faster he goes, the more kinetic energy he gains.

Text-Dependent Questions:

1. What is the gymnastics giant?

2. Is it possible for the gymnast to increase his speed during the giant maneuver? If so, how?

3. What is law of the conservation of energy?

Research Project:

Explore energy transfer with this fun project. Build this simple apparatus. Get two chairs and tie a string between them. Create two pendulums from string tied to an object like a ball made of modeling clay, a rubber ball, or other sphere. Hold one pendulum still and release the other pendulum. While the first pendulum is in motion, release the other pendulum. Record what happens to each pendulum, and explain the results.

WORDS TO UNDERSTAND

moment arm: the length between the axis and application of force point

proprioception: awareness of the position of one's body

torque: something that produces or tends to produce torsion or rotation; the moment of a force or system of forces tending to cause rotation

CHAPTER 5

TORQUE, TIME, AND TUMBLING

Introduction

Now that we've explored some of the other concepts of physics in gymnastics, we simply must learn about torque, which can really affect flips, twists, and landings. Are a flip and a twist really all that different? Yes, and torque makes the difference.

What Is Torque?

Torque is a foundational principle of human movement and one that all athletes—gymnasts in particular—need to understand. All movements generate torque. Torque is best defined as force multiplied by the perpendicular distance from the line of action to the axis of motion.

Torque makes your body become a more effective lever. The door example from an earlier chapter exemplifies torque. Pushing on the door closest to the hinges makes it more difficult to open, but pushing furthest away from the hinge means the heavy door is easy to open. Think of the hinge as the axis of motion. The force is more effective when it is applied further away from the axis. The length between the axis and application of force point is referred to as the **moment arm**.

Gymnasts think of their bodies as a system of muscle levers. They push and pull, and those levers and pulleys react with particular movements. Torque is needed to operate these levers and pulleys. Torque produces rotation, and gymnasts are trained to determine how much torque

Gymnast's bodies are comprised of a system of muscles that act as levers.

they should generate. They also are trained to minimize torque, which helps to minimize injury. Gymnasts eventually learn to make their muscles and joints act in proportion to the torque; this creates **proprioception**, an awareness of the position of one's own body.

Eventually, gymnasts begin to really tune in to their own proprioception. They have an awareness of how fast a spin is and where their body is in relation to the vault, floor, or bar. At first during training, a desire to go faster may create erratic movement patterns for the gymnast.

A flip is rotation about the horizontal (x-) axis, such as a forward or back flip. A twist is rotation about the vertical axis (y-) that runs the length of the body. In a flip with no torque, the gymnast purely goes around the x-axis. The same is true for a rotation about the axis that runs the length of the body (the y-axis).

So How Does Torque Actually Work?

Torque is a rotational force that acts on a point away from the center of mass. When we do the $F=ma$ force calculations, we have a tendency to simplify the objects that we are calculating forces on. In reality, these objects (like gymnasts) have a complex three-dimensional shape, and that is where torque factors in.

Torque is best defined as a force (F) acting on an object at a distance (r) from the axis of rotation. That distance is referred to as the lever arm, as shown in the diagram, which shows the example of turning a wrench.

West Virginia University's Jordan Gillette performs a backflip on the balance beam at a meet in Morgantown, WV.

There is an x- and y-force component that acts on the lever arm (r), but only the force component perpendicular to the lever arm is relevant. The angle between the force and the lever arm is relevant too and is denoted as Ø.

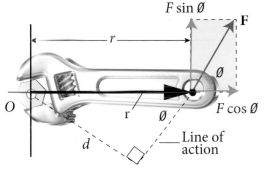

Source: sdsu-physics.org

Here's an example. If the total force acting on the lever arm is 50 Newtons and that force is acting at a 45-degree angle (Ø= 45°) to the lever arm, multiplying 50N by sin (45) will calculate the force needed to rotate the lever arm. In this case, a smaller force of 35N is needed to rotate the body. Now torque has a simpler definition: It is the product of the lever arm distance *r* multiplied by the force acting perpendicular to it.

We can also think of torque as rotational push. The further away from the axis of rotation, the stronger the rotational push. If that same force acts close to the axis of rotation, there is hardly any torque.

Now that we have a basis for torque, let's explore how gymnasts use torque to twist. Torque changes the angular momentum of an object, in this case, a gymnast. If there is no torque on a body, then the angular momentum is constant. We talked about this in the earlier chapter; as the gymnast leaves the ground, there is no torque at that moment.

To perform a twisting maneuver, a gymnast exerts torque by swinging her arms and pushing in opposite directions with her feet as she jumps.

There are three ways to apply torque to a body to create a twist. A torque twist is the simplest way. The gymnast starts a rotation about her body axis by exerting a torque in the same direction. You can't exert a torque when you're in the air, though, so before the gymnast's feet leave the ground, she begins to exert the torque by swinging her arms and pushing forward with one foot and back with the other.

Gymnasts can create rotation to perform twists by moving the top and bottom parts of their bodies in opposite directions in the air.

Gymnasts also do constant angular momentum twists. How? The gymnast leaves the ground with some angular momentum, so a twist can be started by keeping constant angular momentum and without adding any extra torque. How is that possible?

All objects have three axes about which the body can rotate. During flight, the gymnast changes the inertia by moving her arms asymmetrically—pulling one over her head and the other across her torso (or often both across the torso). The arm movement adds torque, and now, the angular momentum is at a different angle because she has changed the angle of rotation. In this way, a gymnast can flip and twist at the same time.

What if a gymnast starts with absolutely no rotation? Can she still twist? Yes! She can rotate one part of the body in one direction and the other part in the opposite direction. Angular momentum is still zero.

 STEM Careers

Are there STEM jobs in gymnastics? Sure there are! You could be an industrial engineer. These engineers make the manufacturing line more efficient. For example, let's say your company is mass-producing balance beams. The industrial engineer looks at the time it takes to perform each step of product assembly. The engineer looks at how quickly and accurately the workers on the manufacturing line can make each balance beam. The engineer is also looking for any problem areas so that the workflow and efficiency of the manufacturing can be improved. The faster the company can make and sell balance beams, the more money it makes. Industrial engineers do math studies called time and motion studies to see how efficient workers are. From these studies, they might change the sequence in which the parts of the balance beam are put together, or they might make sure that materials are more readily available at a particular station to make the job smoother. These engineers must have strong math and statistics skills and a bachelor's degree in engineering. Companies also like industrial engineers to have strong skill sets in computer-aided design software programs.

Tumbling

By now, you have surely done your share of *F=ma* calculations in physics class. A gymnastics tumbling floor routine is a great example of Newton's Second Law of physics. The force exerted on an object is the product of its mass and its acceleration. In the case of a gymnast, the mass is the gymnast's mass. That mass does not change during the floor routine. What does change is the speed at which the gymnast runs across the mat. The faster a gymnast runs, the larger the force applied to the floor. The larger that force, the more force she has to jump in the air and do all those amazing twists and flips.

A tumbling floor is not your typical floor. Competitive gymnastics floors are spring floors, so the larger the force applied downward to the floor, the higher the gymnast goes in the air as she springboards off the mat. Remember, for every action, there is an equal and opposite reaction.

Gymnastics floor routines are performed on spring-supported surfaces that allow gymnasts to gain extra lift when they apply force to that surface.

Vaulting

Gymnasts also sprint in the vault competition. Amazingly, male gymnasts have a short-distance sprint speed of twenty or more miles per hour; women have a sixteen-mile-per-hour run. That's pretty fast! Women and men can reach tumbling and vault heights of thirteen to sixteen feet, respectively.

Researchers have actually studied the vault sprint run. They used high-speed cameras to record the gymnasts. Gymnasts who had peak running speeds scored better in their vaults. Why? Peak speed produced a peak force that allowed them to propel higher in the air and complete more acrobatic elements.

A high-speed run helps a gymnast in the vault event because the gymnast must create sufficient momentum to launch into flight. Coaches train gymnasts to try to consistently reach the maximum running speed they can control. Sure, a gymnast could run faster, but if they can't control the run, they will be unstable on the vault approach. One of the main issues gymnasts have is that they have to attain maximum speed over a very short distance.

Time

Basketball is not the only sport that has hang time. Gymnastics does, too. If you've ever seen a gymnast do a double backflip while standing still, you were probably amazed. The move is extremely difficult, to say the least, but why? First, the backflip is done from a standing position. There is no run up here like in tumbling or the vault. Second, the gymnast must pull his legs into his body as he rotates. You can see that this would be much easier to do as part of a tumbling pass because the gymnast builds speed to create the rotation needed to complete the backflip.

Female gymnasts get up to about 16 mph in the run up to the vault. Gymnasts look for the balance between running fast enough and keeping the speed manageable so they can execute the vault well.

A standing backflip is even more difficult because the gymnast must jump high enough in the air and remain in the air long enough to rotate. That's where hang time comes in. The gymnast needs enough time to rotate twice.

Watch the amazing Aaron Cook perform a standing double backflip.

The gymnast can do maneuvers to help rotation, as shown in the video. You'll notice that Cook swings his arms; this gives him a starting angular momentum. Once Cook is in the air, notice he pulls his legs close to his body. As we learned in earlier chapters, he is redistributing his weight to decrease his rotational mass; when the rotational mass decreases, his rotational speed increases so he can make it twice around.

Cook's hang time in this video is 0.867 seconds. With this hang time, Cook jumps to a height of nearly one meter. This "height" is not the normal height that he jumps from his feet. Instead, this height means that Cook's center of mass increases by one meter in the air as he jumps.

Text-Dependent Questions:

1. How do you define torque?

2. What is proprioception?

3. What makes Aaron Cook's move so difficult?

Research Project:

Calculate your own torque. Choose some different values for total force (such as 80N, 100N, and so on). Next, choose different distance values for r (five inches, twelve inches, and so on). Finally, choose different angles for $\varnothing$ (40°, 55°, 60°, 70°, and so on). Find the resulting torque for several variations. First, find the perpendicular component of force acting on the lever arm.

$F' = $ (total force) $*$ sin $(\varnothing)$
Example: $F' = 80 \text{ N} \cdot \sin (70°) \approx 75.18 \text{ N}$
Next, calculate torque as $T = F' * r$
Example: $T = 0.2 \text{ m} \cdot 75.18 \text{ N} \approx 15.04 \text{ Nm}$
In the example above, what if your resulting torque (T) needed to be higher? What could you do to increase the torque? Log your results, and answers and prepare a short report.

WORDS TO UNDERSTAND

composite: a solid material that is made of two or more substances having different physical characteristics and in which each substance retains its identity while contributing desirable properties to the whole

hygroscopic: readily taking up and retaining moisture

spatial awareness: the ability to see and understand the position of one's own body in relation to other objects

wearables: technology that is worn that connects to the Internet via a wireless Bluetooth connection

CHAPTER 6

HIGH-TECH GYMNASTICS

Introduction

If someone wants to make gymnastics much more difficult, why not just change the equipment to make the sport harder? Great idea—and that's exactly what has happened. Gymnastics has always been a sport that combines athleticism with artistry, but it hasn't always been a serious spectator sport. Did you know that gymnastics was originally created to prepare ancient Greek soldiers for war? It was a mandatory part of their athletic training, and it even made its way to the United States in the 1800s as part of our country's military training. As militaries began to obtain more technology and weapons, gymnastics training was abandoned and replaced by weapons and technology training.

The equipment that we all know and love as gymnastics equipment was invented hundreds of years ago—the balance beam, the rings, the pommel horse, and, of course, the parallel bars. After gymnastics was no longer a part of military training, it began to be developed as its own sport. In 1896, men's gymnastics was included in the first modern Olympic Games.

The gold medal winning team from the Netherlands was the first modern Olympic champion in women's gymnastics.

Women gymnasts first competed in the 1928 Olympics, and the popular floor exercise was added four years later in 1932.

Today, modern gymnastics is definitely a spectator sport, and that is in large part due to the amazing equipment used in the events.

Gymnastic Equipment

Men's gymnastics has six events: floor routine, pommel horse, still rings, vault, parallel bars, and the horizontal bar. Women compete in four events: balance beam, vault, uneven bars, and floor routine. Gymnastics equipment has definitely evolved over time. Let's take a look.

Pommel horse: Interestingly, the Romans originally invented the pommel horse for people to practice dismounting from actual horses. What used to be a simple block of wood with handles evolved to a metal iron frame covered with foam and leather. As gymnastics was originally used by the military, it makes sense that the pommel horse came to be a gymnastics event.

The original pommel horse apparatus was asymmetrical to better resemble a real horse; this type of pommel was used in the 1936 Olympics in Berlin.

In 1948, the Americans introduced a fully symmetrical pommel horse, certified by the International Gymnastics

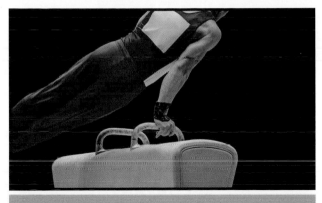

The modern pommel horse is fully symmetrical and constructed with heat molded wood and specialized leather and foam.

Federation in 1956, which has become the standard in gymnastics. The raised handles were added later to allow gymnasts to have more movements. The handles provide the gymnast better support and allow him to make combination moves and to transition between moves.

Modern pommel horses are made of high-performance materials like interior foam to prevent injury and specialized leather that absorbs moisture during competitions. The main body of the pommel horse is made of high-temperature molded wood.

Vaulting table: The vaulting table has perhaps experienced the most dramatic change of all equipment. The original design was a vaulting horse that looked similar to the pommel horse but without handles, but the new design looks like a space age oval landing pad. Gymnasts jokingly call it "the tongue" because that is exactly what it looks like. In the 2000 Olympic Games in Sydney, Australia, many gymnasts had accidents on the old vault design after a setup mistake was made, rendering the

What exactly is a Yurchenko? Find out here.

vault two inches too low. After that, the new design was introduced and is now the standard vault table used for both the men's and women's vault event.

The front face of the vault slopes downward and has thick padding to prevent injuries from accidental collisions. The top of the table also has more padding, and the oval is wider and has a larger surface area, which is more forgiving in case gymnasts are off by a couple of inches. The larger surface area also means that gymnasts can perform more difficult moves. Gymnasts now routinely do handsprings off the vault, and some even do the double twisting back handspring move known as the Yurchenko vault.

The modern vault table is much safer than previous iterations of the apparatus, making it safer for the athletes to attempt the most difficult vaults.

Rings: The rings were invented in the early 1800s and were initially constructed of iron, if you can imagine! A number of different materials have been used since, including rubber, and today for competitions, rings are generally made of wood. The cables attaching the rings to the frame are very high-tech. The cable contains a reflex mechanism attached at the top of the ring tower. The attachment is spring-loaded, meaning that when the gymnast comes down very hard, the cable takes more of the stress impact to relieve the stress on the gymnast's shoulders.

Bars: When first invented, the parallel bars and uneven bars were made of wood. Now, the bars are generally flexible and adjustable and are made of **composite** materials that absorb shock. The bars' material also gives the gymnasts more bounce, and that means they can fly to higher heights.

The uneven bars used to be wood but are now are made of fiberglass with maple wood attached to the outside. They are also now farther apart, and the height of the bars has also been changed to provide better bar clearance.

The high (horizontal) bar used to be a steel bar, and even though it was steel, the bar would still break. Engineers now use a technique called shot peening, a way to cold-work metal to make the steel deform more so that it won't break. Shot peening is similar to sandblasting, where the metal is strengthened and stresses are relieved in the bar.

Balance beam: The balance beam is a relatively new gymnastics event. It didn't appear as a World Championship event until 1934. At that time, beams were only eight centimeters in width, but today they are ten centimeters wide. As gymnasts began doing acrobatics like flips and handsprings on the beam, the beams were reconstructed to be safer and more stable. Modern balance beams have built-in shock-absorbing materials to create less impact on the gymnast's knee, ankle, and hip joints. Beams now have soft end caps to protect gymnasts from hitting their heads on the end of the beam during dismounts. Balance beams also have better grip because they are constructed out of **hygroscopic** material that absorbs water from the surrounding air; it is never wet but provides considerably better grip. Engineers even can engineer the beam to look wider than it actually is, which gives the gymnast more confidence.

Parallel bars are made of a composite material engineered to absorb the shock produced by the powerful maneuvers in modern routines.

STEM Careers

Who makes all that gymnastics equipment? It takes a team of people, but design engineers are key members. Learning to use computer modeling programs is a key element of any design engineer's education. This software allows you to design 3-D models. Let's say you want to design a brand-new vault or pommel horse. Instead of building one straight out, you would use software to come up with your design and modify it. With this software, you can do structural analysis to determine whether the new vault can take the force and loads the gymnasts will place on them. The best part about the software is that you can send the design file to a 3-D printer and come out with your own little minimodel. If you have the chance to take a class in computer modeling software in high school or college, definitely try to do it. Employers look for it.

How Coaches and Athletes Use Technology

Modern computer technology helps both coaches and athletes monitor every aspect of a gymnast's training and performance. **Wearable** technology has transformed the sport. Gymnasts wear motion sensors to record body position while they're in the air. Then, they can compare the actual data to their own sense of **spatial awareness**.

Other wearable technology allows all sorts of parameters to be measured, including acceleration, rotation, and jump height.

Video apps also play a big role. Gymnasts can watch video at regular speed or slow it down or speed it up for greater detail. Athletes can definitely learn and improve this way.

Automated cameras positioned around arenas, like this one at the 2016 Alina Cup Grand Prix in Moscow, capture video of the athlete performing routines from several angles that can be combined to give coaches a detailed frame-by-frame look at performances.

New medical equipment is available for faster detection of injuries, and state-of-the-art braces help with healing time and prevent reinjury.

Laser Judges?

Could lasers replace gymnastics judges? Maybe. The Japanese Gymnastics Association teamed up with Fujitsu Laboratories to create a new 3-D laser sensor system that helps with scoring during gymnastics competitions. They invented it because gymnastics is becoming so much more advanced, some feel judges are having a harder time catching everything and accurately judging just using the naked eye.

Gymnastics judges may soon have the support of a 3-D laser sensor system to help improve their accuracy.

Fujitsu designed the program with its own data-processing system to be able to analyze proper technique and provide feedback to the judges. This way, the judges can see how close they were to accurately scoring performances.

Many judges have been criticized and even banned for biased scoring. Human scoring is difficult because judges have to make split-second decisions. In a recent research study, data showed that even the best international judges catch only 40 percent of true errors.

There is now 3-D software that uses motion-capture technology to help eliminate bias. Laser measurements are made during each performance that focus on the accuracy of the technique and the difficulty of the routine. The idea of using a system like this has not been popular or widely adopted because sensors and equipment are needed all over the gym floor, thereby getting in the way of gymnasts while doing their routines.

This new system uses miniaturized wireless technology. The Japanese team plans to test the technology's accuracy using real data from Japanese gymnasts. If it passes muster, Japan will use it in real time at low-level competitions in Japan to put it to the test. If all goes as planned Japan is hoping that it will be fully developed to use at the 2020 Olympic Games in Tokyo.

What Are You Wearing?

Wearable technology changed the 2016 Olympics. The US Olympic Committee (USOC) decided to bring in wearable tech for sports like gymnastics, boxing, diving, cycling, wrestling, track and field, and many others. The technology allowed coaches and athletes to gain insight from data that was previously inaccessible. Boxers had insight on their punching speed. Divers and gymnasts wore sensors to determine how high they jumped and how long it took them to get into their first spin. It was a huge boost in learning and taught the athletes invaluable information about their own spatial awareness, and the athletes improved their performance—mathematically!

Building a Better Gymnast

Gymnastics scoring is brutal. One-tenth of a point can make a difference in the medal you receive. Gymnasts want the latest technology to close that gap, and the US Olympic Center is meeting that demand.

One of the things they've worked on is a way for gymnasts to hold their legs just a bit higher. In order to do that, the muscles in the leg must be really well stretched. Their research shows that placing the leg on a vibrating surface during stretching leads to greater flexibility. The vibrating surface is nicknamed "the box." It is shaped

Video technology detected a flaw in the surface that was causing injuries in the floor exercise.

like a miniature pommel horse and shakes at a frequency of 30 Hertz. Male gymnasts have shown a whopping 400 percent improvement in muscle flexibility. So have skaters, swimmers, and divers.

The USOC has also worked with gymnasts to refine their takeoff techniques on the vault run-up and when tumbling on the spring floor. After several injuries, the USOC took high-speed footage of the athletes running. At 500 frames per second, the system takes a lot of images that were then reviewed frame by frame. It was discovered that the injured athletes were making a slight adjustment on the last down/up step on their run. It was so slight that the naked eye couldn't see it, and the athletes didn't even know they were doing it until they saw their own footage.

Right before launching off the floor and onto the vault or into their tumbling passes, the athletes were making this inefficient motion. Why? It turns out the spring floor was not properly bending. In a normal run, the floor should go down when the athlete goes down and go up when the athlete goes up. The floor was going up when the athlete was going down, and that led to a waste in energy in the added move. Over time, the floor design was putting a lot of extra strain on the gymnasts' legs. Sure enough, many of the injuries were ruptured Achilles tendons caused by repetitive motion injury due to the floor.

Pressure Map

The USOC also uses embedded floor technology to map the pressures that gymnasts apply to the floor during takeoff. Since you can't use a regular rigid force plate under a spring floor, the USOC developed technology that the athlete wears on the foot. Amazingly, more than 1,000 sensors are placed on each foot. These sensors provide a continuous color-coded pressure map of the foot plants of each gymnast. Data shows that gymnasts often rely on one foot more than the other. We all have a "dominant" leg, and in certain situations some gymnasts also relied on a noninjured leg. The data has been priceless to coaches in helping gymnasts perfect their form.

Nike invented a special foot device called the Pidima (Greek for "leap") just for the vault. The device looks like a sock or slipper and is intended to help gymnasts stick their landings.

Text-Dependent Questions:

1. What was the pommel horse used for prior to gymnastics?

2. What was the primary reason for completely redesigning the vault apparatus?

3. How did wearable technology change the 2016 Olympic Games for American athletes?

Research Project:

Choose an existing piece of gymnastics equipment. What design improvements would you make to it for safety or better athletic performance? If you had to design a whole new gymnastics event, what would it be, and how would you design the equipment for it? Draw a sketch of your improved design to include with your event proposal.

WORDS TO UNDERSTAND

macronutrients: a nutrient that is needed in large amounts to be essential to growth and health; examples are carbohydrates, fats, and proteins

plyometrics: exercises that involve repeated rapid stretching and contracting of muscles to increase muscle power; examples include jumping and rebounding

strength-to-weight ratio: a material's or person's strength divided by its density

CHAPTER 7

TRAINING, FITNESS, AND NUTRITION

Introduction

Nutrition, training, and fitness can make the difference between being an average athlete and a superior athlete. In the first chapter, we discussed how well-rounded gymnasts have to be. They need strength, speed, rhythm, and so much more. Every day, the bar is being raised higher for gymnasts—no pun intended—so they need the best approaches to fitness to stay competitive.

In general, female gymnasts are small, lean, and very muscular. These ladies have a high power-to-weight ratio and are generally in peak form in their late teens to early twenties. Male gymnasts also tend to be smaller and leaner but are heavily muscled; gymnasts are usually in peak condition in their twenties because muscle mass generally peaks at that age.

Training

At a minimum, gymnasts typically train for a minimum of three hours per training session, at least three times per week. Elite Olympians can train for more than thirty hours a week, morning

Both male and female gymnasts are typically short, but heavily muscled.

and night, during competition season. The training encompasses a broad array of skills, such as strength training and flexibility training. Many gymnasts train in ballet for precision step work.

Most male gymnasts weigh less than 150 pounds, but they appear to weigh much more based on their massively muscular upper bodies. With all that muscle, a male gymnast's body is very lean, which makes their muscle size appear to be even larger. They don't have bulk, though, meaning that despite their ripped muscles, male gymnasts don't look like body builders. Think about it this way: Gymnasts work on every part of their body every day, whereas body builders tend to do repetitions just on a specific muscle to build bulk. This explains why gymnasts have overall lean body looks.

Some male gymnasts have longer, leaner body types, whereas others have heavier, more muscular body types. The same is true for female gymnasts, and either way, most gymnasts—male or female—have very little body fat. Their physical training is so intense and they use so much energy during training that their bodies are very efficient at burning fat for fuel. Overall weight is not so important, because they typically have tremendous strength for their body weights. However, gymnasts closely monitor their percentage of body fat.

A lean body weight is ideal for optimum performance in gymnastics because it allows the athlete to maximize his or her **strength-to-weight ratio**. But what exactly is lean muscle mass, and why is it important?

It makes sense to say that muscle size is directly proportional to muscle strength, known as contractile strength. The bigger the muscle, the stronger it is. Gymnasts must do a coordinated set of movements that effectively transfer energy from the muscles into the upper and lower body for maximum performance on the vault, beam, or bars.

Lean body mass is a measurement of how much nonfat mass your body has. Let's say you have two 200-pound individuals. One has a 30 percent body fat measurement whereas the other, leaner person has

Gymnasts' bodies are very efficient at burning fat for fuel, so they have a very low percentage of body fat.

10 percent. The effective mass of the first person is 140 pounds, but the second person's mass is effectively 180 pounds. Which has the potential for a higher strength-to-weight ratio?

As the saying goes, "mass equals gas," but just because you have muscle mass does not necessarily mean you have strength, and that's where the training comes in! Taller gymnasts have extra body weight, so they must be strong enough to handle the extra pounds.

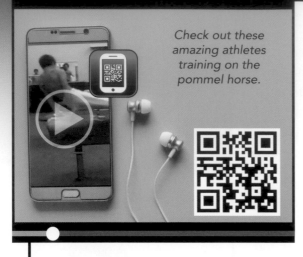

Check out these amazing athletes training on the pommel horse.

How do gymnasts train to build lean mass? Do they focus on weight lifting, or do they use other techniques? Most gymnastic training uses body-weight-only exercises and **plyometric** movements. Many add ankle weights or wrist weights to their training, or add a weighted training vest to increase the weight being lifted. Gymnasts also do single-legged and single-arm exercises for intensity training and to correlate their movements to become more specific. Rather than just doing reps, gymnasts focus on how well the exercise is performed.

Flexibility and mobility training is key for both male and female gymnasts. These exercises are designed to elongate muscle fibers so that they're stretched out to maximum effect. All gymnasts must have a certain strength-to-weight ratio. This allows them to safely perform the gymnastics maneuvers with maximum muscle power.

During the course of their training, gymnasts naturally develop leg strength. They typically spend much more time developing the upper body. If you think about it, a gymnast's shoulders perform the function of hips in many cases because of their acrobatic moves. This is why gymnasts are known for their broad, enormous shoulders.

Also keep in mind that gymnasts are training for multiple events. Some gymnasts compete in all events for a shot at the best all-around gymnast title. Isn't it amazing to think about a single athlete being so diverse as to excel in all of these events? Other gymnasts choose to specialize in certain events. "Leg" events are the vault and the floor exercises; "arm" events are the rings and bar events.

Gymnasts do lots of abdominal work to strengthen the core muscles of the torso. Exercises like Pilates require gymnasts to equally balance both sides of their bodies and to learn to stabilize their body weight.

Morning workouts typically include conditioning and basic exercises, whereas evening workouts typically work on specific skills. The gymnast will run through his or her routines and focus much more on flexibility.

Gymnasts often have additional workouts to focus on weight training or cardio training. At the highest level, they typically work out six days a week for multiple workouts per day. Training is maximized during competitions, but after they're over, coaches usually reduce training to allow the gymnasts' bodies some much-needed recuperation time. During the off-season, gymnasts tend to focus on strength training and conditioning.

Gymnastics training naturally builds powerful legs, like those of Olympic champion Aly Raisman of the US.

The Science of Body-Weight Training

Gymnasts rarely lift weights. Their strength comes from years of dedicated body-weight training. This means doing exercises that use the body to provide resistance. Why does it work? Progressively increasing the repetitions in exercises like push-ups and pull-ups will force the body to synthesize more protein to adapt to the increasing demand. This results in the body adding more muscle tissue to keep up. The movements of gymnastics routines require that gymnasts move on all three geometric planes: the coronal (side to side), the sagittal (front to back), and the transversal (rotating). Therefore the training reflects this required range of motion. Don't believe the science? Next time you watch gymnastics, just look at the muscles that can come from using your body as the barbell.

Gymnasts typically divide workouts into ones that focus on conditioning and those that work on skills and flexibility.

Nutrition

Imagine how much energy you would need to do all those flips and vaults. Gymnasts do need a lot of calories, but intake, of course, depends on the individual person. Calories should always be from a balanced, nutritious diet. Gymnasts must consume enough food each day to maintain body weight and lean mass.

Food intake is divided into categories called **macronutrients**, meaning the amount of protein, fats, and carbohydrates the body needs to function. Carbohydrates are very important for gymnasts to maintain their energy levels. Glycogen is stored as carbohydrates in muscles, and a gymnast's body uses those glycogen stores to power through workouts and competitions. Therefore, a gymnast's diet is about 60 percent carbohydrates. Fat should also be part of the diet but limited to 20 percent or less. Protein should make up the other 20 percent; protein is important because gymnasts need it to repair tissue and muscle damage.

Coaches recommend three meals a day, plus snacks for gymnasts particularly preworkout snacks like muffins, peanut butter on toast, or yogurt.

Text-Dependent Questions:

1. Why is strength-to-weight ratio so important for a gymnast?

2. What is lean body mass?

3. What is a macronutrient? Give three examples that you eat in your diet.

Research Project:

Make up different gymnast body profiles. Make some tall and skinny, and make some short and more bulky. Have fun with it. Research typical bench press weights that athletes can lift—for example, athletes can bench press 250, 300, and more pounds. Calculate the strength-to-weight ratios of your various athletes by dividing strength (the amount they can bench press) by their body weight. What did you learn?

Acceleration - the rate of change of velocity with respect to time.

Aerodynamics - the branch of mechanics that deals with the motion of air and other gases, and with the effects of such motion on bodies in the medium.

Algorithm - a set of rules for solving a problem in a finite number of steps.

Amplitude - the absolute value of the maximum displacement from a zero value during one period of an oscillation.

Analytics - the analysis of data, typically large sets of business data, by the use of mathematics, statistics, and computer software.

Biometrics - Methods for differentiating humans based on one or more intrinsic physical or behavioral traits such as fingerprints or facial geometry.

Center of gravity - the point at which the entire weight of a body may be considered as concentrated so that if supported at this point the body would remain in equilibrium in any position.

Force - strength or energy exerted or brought to bear.

Geometry - the part of mathematics concerned with the size, shape, and relative position of figures, or the study of lines, angles, shapes, and their properties.

Inertia - the property of matter by which it retains its state of rest or its velocity along a straight line so long as it is not acted on by an external force.

Kinetic energy - energy associated with motion.

Mass - the quantity of matter as determined from its weight.

Parabola - a type of conic section curve, any point of which is equally distant from a fixed focus point and a fixed straight line.

Potential energy - the energy of a body or system as a result of its position in an electric, magnetic, or gravitational field.

Velocity - rapidity of motion or operation; swiftness; speed.

FURTHER READING

Meyers, Dvora. *The End of the Perfect 10: The Making and Breaking of Gymnastics' Top Score—from Nadia to Now.* Touchstone Press, 2016.

USA Gymnastics. USA Gymnastics: Weight Management, Nutrition, and Energy Needs For Gymnastics. https://usagym.org/PDFs/Home/120610_weightmanagement.pdf

The Collegiate and Professional Sports Dieticians Association. *Nutrition for the Gymnastics Student Athlete*, 2015. http://www.sportsrd.org/wp-content/uploads/2015/01/Gymnastics_Sports_Nutrition_web.pdf

Savage, Jeff. *Top 25 Gymnastics Skills, Tips, and Tricks.* Enslow Publishers, 2011.

Morgan, Elizabeth. *Gymnastics: Science on the Mat and in the Air.* Science Behind Sports. Lucent Books, 2017.

INTERNET RESOURCES

The official website of gymnast Olga Korbut:
http://olgakorbut.com/

The official website of Simone Biles.
http://www.simonebiles.com/

American Society of Mechanical Engineers (ASME) talks about flipping over high-tech gymnastics.
https://www.asme.org/engineering-topics/articles/design/flipping-for-hightech-gymnastics

Wearable. Rio Olympics 2016: How wearable tech will power Team U.S.A. to golds galore.
https://www.wareable.com/sport/wearable-tech-at-rio-olympics-2016-2097.

INDEX

INDEX

AUTHOR BIOGRAPHY

Jacqueline Havelka is a rocket scientist turned writer. She is a biomedical engineer with a degree from Texas A&M University, and worked at Lockheed Martin as an aerospace contractor for the NASA Johnson Space Center in Houston, Texas. In her twenty-five-year career, she managed space life sciences experiments and data for the International Space Station & Space Shuttle. She began work on Shuttle mission STS-40 and worked until the last Shuttle launch of STS-135. While at NASA, she served in technical lead and management roles. She was a charter designer of the NASA Life Sciences Data Archive, a repository of NASA human, animal, and biological research from the Gemini program to present day.

In 2017, she founded her own company to provide medical and technical freelance writing to clients. She has always had the desire to start her own business, and she loves the challenge and diversity of international projects that her new business brings. She learns something new every single day, and that is a very good thing.

EDUCATIONAL VIDEO LINKS

Pg. 13: http://x-qr.net/1Kxq
Pg. 21: http://x-qr.net/1J8A
Pg. 26: http://x-qr.net/1JPY
Pg. 35: http://x-qr.net/1KQd
Pg. 37: http://x-qr.net/1LdH

Pg. 42: http://x-qr.net/1Kkx
Pg. 44: http://x-qr.net/1LAE
Pg. 54: http://x-qr.net/1JSf
Pg. 60: http://x-qr.net/1M4h
Pg. 72: http://x-qr.net/1M0s

PICTURE CREDITS